A STROKE
OF LUCK

CHRIS BENNETT

authorHOUSE®

AuthorHouse™ UK
1663 Liberty Drive
Bloomington, IN 47403 USA
www.authorhouse.co.uk
Phone: 0800.197.4150

Published by AuthorHouse 09/23/2016

ISBN: 978-1-5246-6306-3 (sc)
ISBN: 978-1-5246-6305-6 (hc)
ISBN: 978-1-5246-6307-0 (e)

Print information available on the last page.

Any people depicted in stock imagery provided by Thinkstock are models,
and such images are being used for illustrative purposes only.
Certain stock imagery © Thinkstock.

This book is printed on acid-free paper.

CONTENTS

A NOTE FROM THE AUTHOR

In everything I have said and done in this book, it comes from the heart. I would not wish to offend anyone and I can assure you that has never been my intention. My blockage/Stroke/Brain Injury/ Infarction has been a journey, one of soul searching, tears, anxiety, being scared and frightened because of the unknown.

I understand that every stroke is different and how it leaves a person varies; I am not medically trained and can only give an account of my own Stroke. Remember, what-ever you are feeling, what-ever you are going through there are people out there who do understand.

From seeing others, to experiencing a stroke, the love, words and support of others will get you through but the feeling of having another, they tell me will fade in time.

Dear reader I hope my words and story have helped. All as I can say, it gets easier over time. Keep going and live each day for yourself and others and take each day slowly. Let's face it I cannot run a marathon just yet, but who knows in time..

With Kindest Wishes

Chris Bennett

INTRODUCTION

The stroke I am referring to in this book is a CVA (Cerebrovascular Accident). In my case a blockage in the central lobe with banging headache, dizziness and then the whole left side with no feeling. Not nice! However, with the help love and support of others and one year on. I can now share my story with others. Who knows it may help others to cope. If they can read, (I know mine affected my vision), so perhaps an audio version, or someone to read for you.

My concentration levels were not good at first. I knew, I needed to keep my brain active; I did not want to lose my mind, memory etc. I realised this was life threating when my Consultant turned to my Husband and said "we need to do it quickly; time is not on her side." My husband's response was "don't stand there, get on with it." And my life from now on would be different.

Through this book I am going to share my deepest darkest days, and explain to you while I feel lucky.

I need to say 'Thank you,' for the love, support shared by my husband, Mick, and for making me get out there and do things; including going with me to my Stroke support group. Our children: Michelle, Clare, Gemma and Mike: Their other halves: Rob, Colin, Jade, and Gavin. Our marvellous Grand children who really keep me motivated and getting me back to some normality: Ben, Isabelle, Seth and Henry.

To the support of my sister: Lesley and her other half Peter (whom if it was not for him this would have not been published – so a BIG thank you, and our great friends; Martyn and Tracey, they have always been there for us.

The Stroke Group; Michelle the organiser and all our friends we have made: you are all marvellous and such an inspiration.

Lastly, but not at all least, to you dear readers; for taking the time to read my story. I hope that this will give you inspiration and to live your life day, by, day and enjoy the joys around us.

Thank you Chris Bennett

CHAPTER 1
EXPLAINING TO THE PROFESSIONALS

It was a year ago today; as I said those words and I looked around the room. On both sides of me I knew I had support from Michelle, community stoke organiser and another young Stroke victim; Michelle had just introduced me to her, (she had a stroke 4 years ago whilst pregnant with her first child). The shock she was still coming to terms with. Was mine not as bad, was it harder for her, or was it that I had that extra; love support and encouragement I needed. This is me now a year on; my foot, at times will drag, my knee gives away, my speech will slur when I am tired, but I still have this head!

When I say I have this head, I mean, I know I have the same initial pain as two days post stoke. I do get some relief from a slow release pain killer, which I had recommended to me and would recommend to others, (by word of mouth) as I do not want to get in trouble, or be sued by any pharmaceutical company. So I will not divulge until I have permission. However, just to say I take it at 8 o'clock in the morning and then again at 8pm. If I don't, I feel like someone has cuffed me around the back of the head, (my husband hates me using this term, he says it sounds like I hit you), in which I can honestly say this has never happened. Still the more I think about professionals: Consultants, Doctors, Nurses, and share this with them they just say 'yes, and you have the painkillers'. I tell you I could scream, does no one listen, I don't want painkillers I want it to go.

One in ten people have pain after stroke, neuropathic pain as I understand. At my follow up appointment I was told it was because of the damage to the brain. (I know I have **Brain Damage**), great anything else! Ok, but why the pain. She went onto explain that part of the brain where the blockage was found has been damaged, so the rest of the brain is trying to compensate. So why is it I still have numbness, pins and needles, pain! It needs to repair. How long! They don't know, but I can tell you a year on the symptoms are getting better, yes, I am on tablets, but feeling better.

So as I lay in bed with no feeling on my left hand side and given a bed pan to pee in, have they tried this with no feeling on your left side. I was lucky to have feeling in my bladder yes, but trying to slide it underneath sit on top of it and pee. Well that was it when I got there and managed to pee in the pan, I reached out for my button and it slid off the bed. Why hadn't anyone helped me, why hadn't they asked? But then OAP's where on the wonder.

I know we all have to get old, but awake all night and snore all day. It was like the waking of the zombies as they all drifted and moaned around the ward. I could not move, but why were they are on the move. I thought this was a stroke ward. The hours ticked by slowly, I must have had about an hour of sleep, then I started to think what next and then it stuck me. **"I am lucky, I am alive!"** I tried to lift my body with my right side and lift my body all in one movement. You can guess what happened. Yes, I ended up with wet sheets!

Or the joys, the indignity. I know they get busy at night, but this was ridiculous. Just a little help that's all. I waited until I could hear one of them walk through, it seemed ages. When they came I called and apologised, why! They left me o' well, I know there are other patients but I was soon taken care of, and back to sleep; apart from the checking, the temperature blood pressure etc, half hourly, hourly so not much sleep as you can image.

The hours turned into days and the days turned into nights until I slowly had movement in my left hand. It started to feel like a ton weight what is happening, is the feeling really coming back? It was another few days and the arm and foot retained some normality. Pins and needles, numbness and can I walk? Encouragement from the Physiotherapy team and having to say 'British Constitutional' several times! It is something to do with the sounds. Can anyone say this even if they have not had a stroke?

The brain was good I passed a test to see how competent I was. Just forgot one thing, that's not bad. They were happy to release me home with after care. That's another chapter.

NOTES

_____

_____

_____

_____

_____

_____

_____

_____

_____

_____

_____

Chris Bennett

_____

_____

_____

_____

_____

_____

_____

_____

_____

Chris Bennett

CHAPTER 2
QUICK THINKING PROFESSIONALS

First of all what happened to me I would not wish to happen to anyone. I had suffered with high blood pressure for some time; this was being monitored and checked regularly at my GP Surgery. Cholesterol; healthy diet tick, low fat spread tick, 5 a day tick, cakes and saturated fat, mmm! I do like sweets and cakes but I do try hard to eat them as a treat. Alcohol (not on a school night), the odd glass at weekends, and a few more on holidays. Over-weight, well I could do with being a stone lighter. That's pretty much it heath wise. Oh! I have hay fever in the summer months but all under control or so I thought.

Monday 29th June, 2015, it was our twins' birthday they were thirty-one. I had text them both and at 7am picked up my bags I had prepared for the day and went to the garage. I had been suffering from a headache all weekend; it was that bad that I had to take Friday off, (first day off sick in 2 years). Not like you, my TA's (Teaching Assistants) said, get well soon. As I bent down to open the garage door I became dizzy and shook my head. Come on I said to myself. the children need you today, I need to teach! Little did I know then that it is still not possible.

As I drove the car down the driveway my vision became blurred and I was seeing double. I pulled the car to one side and parked so others could get in and out the driveway. I closed my eyes the head and dizziness was even more apparent. I managed to get out of the car and go indoors. I said to my husband that I really was not feeling well and was not sure if it was my blood pressure. Having no apparent previous symptoms, I was not sure.

The Doctors was some forty minutes away from where I live. The appointment was made. I cannot remember the time now. I remember my husband saying our son is off I'll phone him.. On phoning him he was in the car the traffic was building up. He made the journey both ways. We arrived seven minutes late but the Doctor agreed to see me. She was a locum (who has since, I am pleased to say a permanent member of staff). On looking at me and asking my symptoms, she said "if you were in A & E now we would be giving you an injection." Before I could even ask what it was for, this was done.

After a few minutes I explained that I was seeing six of her, I think we need to lay you down was the reply. My son came in. I will always remember in this other Nurses room the screen was on and there were penguins. I pointed this out to my son, as he loves penguins. Ever since being a small child. (I recall one time we visit London Zoo and stood watching them for an hour, our other children asked to go but still he would not move). I counted the penguins 1, 2, 3, 4, 5, 6. Look 6 penguins. My sons exact words I hope I can repeat were "mum are you pissed!"

He obviously became concerned when I went no, but wow! I have a strange feeling, I cannot feel the side of my face, (before he could reply) now my arm, my leg and my foot. I remember describing it to him and it is still so vivid. Many say they cannot remember, I still refer this as a wave to my Consultants. Two people I have known from my stroke club have described theirs' in the same way.

By know my son was concerned and as he stood up the Doctor came in. "How are you feeling now Mrs Bennett?" I cannot feel my left side, I replied. "I think you have had a Stroke Mrs Bennett?" I am calling the team at the hospital and an ambulance. I looked at my son and said no old people have these. He smiled. I replied "I am not that old."

When the ambulance came to me, the Paramedics did their checks and were not sure if I had a stroke. I remember being quickly wheeled into the ambulance and the nice young man pulled me over to the chair. I still could not feel a thing; my dizziness was still there, my head pounding. What was happening? My son went to get my husband. With blues and twos going through the school traffic I was there in no time and being assessed.

My husband came in and with an enigmatic smile could not believe what he was witnessing. I was prodded from my arm down to my toes, no reflexes, nothing on my left side. All as I kept thinking was it will pass. (I have tried to explain the feeling to others. No feeling of numbness. you just cannot move). The Consultant was called in minutes and I was whisked off for a CT scan. He was very reassuring and said I had done well and he would see me shortly. What did that mean?

When I arrived back in Rhesus the Consultant was talking with my husband and I heard him say "We are running out of time and not sure if it will work." My husband turned to him and said "don't waste time, get on with it."

I had a line put in and another with the 'drain unblocker,' sorry: I was Thromberlised. This takes one hour for this liquid to circulate the body. Still very light headed, like I had been drinking.. No! Not a drop all weekend. This amazing clot busting drug was great. It would mean being monitored for seventy-two hours; not sure if it was every thirty minutes or every hour. I was forever having my blood pressure taken, fluids checked and temperature. I understand your temperature and pressures change with this drug.

When things had calmed down my husband was aloud in and my Consultant stood and explained that I had a Stroke, caused by a blockage in my central lobe. The drug (which is not used in many hospitals has to be administered within a short space of time). It appeared that as I could pinpoint my time the drug could be used. The regular monitoring continued.

It was the third day when I woke up and could move my fingers. This was very pleasing to all. Slowly during the day more movement was apparent. Although, my limbs felt that they were being pressed down and I was lifting weights. From that time on physiotherapists, Orthopaedics and nurses, Consultants and his team buzzed around me. It was like a whirl wind approaching and circling. Others on the ward who had all suffered and some who seemed to be asleep all day and come alive at night were asking questions. At one point I just wanted to sleep, however, I had the reassuring visits from husband, family and friends that kept me going.

I just wanted to keep my mind active. I asked my husband to bring up puzzle books and was determined not to lose my mind/brain activity. I was not allowed to eat until they have checked my swallowing and said 'British Constitutional' (as mentioned before). Things were coming back to life slowly as well as other patients. As I said before the elderly in my stroke ward used to wander around and keep everyone awake. It was something like the wakening a Robin Williams film as I recall.

Any way all joking aside I was lucky. As I came to the end of that speech/talk I gave a year later and said I was lucky 'To Be Alive!'

Thank you NHS.

NOTES

Chris Bennett

_____

_____

_____

_____

_____

_____

_____

_____

_____

_____

_____

Chris Bennett

CHAPTER 3
AFTER CARE

I still could not really take in what had happened to me. My husband kept checking on me, my family and friends. How are you feeling? They would ask. I still had this pounding head, heavy arms and legs and could not pick my foot up from the floor without dragging it.

My husband would say we needed to get out for a walk. I would cling onto him and drag my foot. The movement would be slow and to get to the end of the driveway seemed to take forever. I would get back exhausted and need to sleep. I would sit there in floods of tears. My family would telephone and I would say I am ok, I am getting there. But I could tell they were all so worried. I needed to be checked by the consultant and visit my Doctor for a certificate. I knew I would not be back at work like this. How long for I did not know.

My left eye started to go twitchy and blurry. What on earth was going on? My head still pounding, my tongue numb and constant pins and needles. That's good they would say, it's all coming back. This feeling of being worthless would not go away. I tried to manipulate my hands and fingers of my left hand. I was determined to concentrate on something. I started knitting again. This was really slow and the weakness in my left hand was really slow going, but I would not give up.

The tears still flowed; I tried to clean my bathroom. I had managed to get down on my hands and knees and could not get up. I felt so tied. I just sat in the middle of the bathroom floor and just cried. My husband heard me and trying to keep a brave face, said "come on you daft thing, get up!" He went to pull me up and touched my left side I jumped anyone touching this in the early days seemed to leave a lasting impression. Is this my life now is this how it is going be?

Six weeks from my stroke I had an appointment, the following week I was away to Malta on holiday. Movement was there, I still could not bear the touch on my left side, but I was determined to go. It had been booked and paid for the last eight months. What would the consultant say?

Yes, you can fly.. (As the words were said they echoed around the room all the fears of the last six weeks had gone the anxiety of what might happen next). We both sat there and smiled. You will need physiotherapy, the other symptoms will improve. You have had a brain injury, the parts where you had the block are dead, other pathways will develop as it repairs. We will see you again soon. Just how soon I had no idea, but I had something to concentrate on my holiday.

There was one piece of good advice the Consultant gave me, make sure you rest when your body tells you and you must drink plenty of water. So we packed for our holiday.

I did not think it would be slow going climbing up the steps of the plane, but as always I was so determined. Tied yes, but tried to keep going as much as I could. We walked further each day, I got into the pool in the villa and swam but not for long. Drank plenty of water and took my prescribed medication. Everything was going well until the end of the week. My ankles started to hurt and swell. My husband worried as ever bless him, found the nearest Doctors, they informed me that I would have to rest put my feet up and keep them cool out of the sun. That was fine but the passing line was, "if the swelling has not reduced by tomorrow you need to come to the hospital.

The rest of the day we sat in the shade, at night time my feet where raised and we rested. The next day they had gone down but my husband insisted we stayed at the villa. By the second day they had returned to normal and I am pleased to say we enjoyed the rest of the holiday.

Although, sleeping was a problem, it was hot even with the fans, (no air conditioning, until we got to our hotel for the second week). We would often be up having a cup of tea and playing cards at 2am in the morning.

The fortnight soon went, the tears were less and I felt more relaxed. The heaviness and movement was a little better and I could raise my foot a little more. I tried to do my own exercise and the knitting continued. At least my Granddaughter and Daughter benefited from my therapy. Still no physiotherapy, my own exercises continued. We would go out for a longer walk each day and take each day at a time.

My husband would go over to our club twice a week, each time asking me if I would go. I did not want to; I did not want people seeing me a shadow of my former self. I did not realise how isolated I was becoming. Our friends would come over and in the early days take me to the hospital and doctors. I had attended the eye clinic and was told part of my peripheral inner vision had gone. But who goes looking around at their own nose all day. I had the words said "you can drive, this would not stop you". My husband's outer peripheral vision had gone a few years before and he had to give up driving so it was like music to our ears.

Our children did not like the idea of me driving but I wanted to. I was fine but could not go too far and my husband said no not after 2pm as I get so tied. This has improved after a year. I still get tired but I still drive better than I walk.

The days went by and the end of August was soon arriving. I felt really tied this particular day, and not right. I lay on the settee in my nightie as I often did. It would take me a while to get to sleep and even longer trying to get myself alert. I got up after about an hour and went to the bedroom. I often needed help putting my arms in clothes; bad arm first we used to say; then my cropped trousers, (bad leg first). I was once asked how I managed with my bra; how I always do it, put the fastening in the front do up and turn, (a hard job), I would say at least half an hour getting dressed with help. But this got less as time went on, and now well I could probably race you but might need to sit down for half an hour after.

As this would wear me out I returned to the settee as usual. My husband gave me lunch and I had been doing some knitting. I then alerted him to the pains I was having in my chest and going across, then my legs and arms. The shooting pain was going right across my body. Would this ever stop! Worried he contacted our son. He said get an ambulance. We were taken to the local hospital and a Stroke Nurse came to see me. She asked what were my symptoms, and I said it's not like before. I have this electric shook type pain, but I still have a pounding head. We need to take you to the CT scanner and see what is happening. As I lay in the scanner it brought all the memories back. Suddenly my left side had gone again. No pain! No feeling!. Tears running down my face; "Mrs Bennett what-ever is wrong?"

Thirty-six hours later I could move my hand and slowly my arm and foot. Was this another stroke? An MRI scan revealed a flair. What was a flair? The physiotherapist: Harold came around to see me. Come on Mrs Bennett we are going to get out of bed.

I started to try and stand with support I managed this and then my leg I pushed and dragged my foot along the floor. All what I had been through, what for, it just was not fair. Why me? The tears started again and if by magic my husband was there. We have done this before we will do it again he said.

The Consultant came around and introduced me to a Neurologist. We have looked at your scans, you can go home, you have had a flair. The physiotherapist is coming back to see me today. Oh, don't worry we will sort visits and you will see the physio soon.

Six weeks later the Neurologist who talked about the flair said it is where the brain heals. I mentioned I was getting more pain than ever. This was Neuropathic pain and these tablets would help. More tablets? How many more did I have to take?

Where was the Physiotherapy? What about my draggy foot? The pain? Too many questions on top of this I felt more isolated. Nobody had seen me at home; surely there should be some form of after care. To treat my mind, body and soul!

I heard that another friend who lived near me, a lot older had had a stroke. He was getting a lot of physiotherapy, support. Where was mine?

My husband phoned the hospital, stroke ward and asked for a local number for nursing care, who could give me some support. The stroke association had a local nurse who visited homes for after care. Michelle South-West Stroke Co-ordinator came to see me several times and mentioned a club she had formed, we sat and talked but I was reluctant to attend a club with others. I joked with my son and said it would be like 'Alcoholics anonymous,' no disrespect to them, I hear they do a wonderful job.

I finally went, with my husbands' support it was the best thing I have ever done. To talk with others who understand how I was feeling. We shared our frustrations and the triumphs'; getting my reflexes back in left side to walking and lifting my leg. Finally, others had been through the same as myself, two or three years on some more recent.

Yes, the first visit was "Hi I am Chris, I have had a stroke." After that initial line I felt at ease and we chatted for two hours and now they are our friends. My husband found other halves to talk to. They share ideas of how they all cope. We have even done a stroke walk, supporting each other and raised £150.00 for the Stroke Association. We meet every two weeks and it has been the best tonic ever. Then I was asked to share my story and help others. First an NHS meeting and now a befriender at our club; Who knows what the future holds? The support of others at different stages of their strokes, I am so lucky to have a group like this. Thank you Michelle.

Physiotherapy, well that's the next chapter a story within its' self.

NOTES

Chris Bennett

_____

_____

_____

_____

_____

_____

_____

_____

_____

_____

_____

_____

_____

Chris Bennett

Chris Bennett

_____

_____

_____

_____

_____

_____

_____

_____

_____

_____

_____

CHAPTER 4
PHYSIOTHERAPY

After the flair (something to do with fluid levels in the brain, but I am not medically trained and will leave that to the professionals); my leg and foot were not right. As I said before when I was discharged from hospital the Consultant had said the Physiotherapy would be in touch. I phoned physiotherapy every week but still no referral. The weeks turned into a month. I telephoned the Consultant's secretary to be told the referral had been made weeks previously. Again I phoned physiotherapy again nothing. I left this another week and telephoned again. Nothing!

I was getting so frustrated by now that in desperation I telephone the Neurologist secretary, in tears and left a message on the answer tape. A telephone call within the next hour assured me that the letter had been retyped and she was just waiting for the Consultant to sign for the referral. I had been told previously that an electronic referral is made. Anyway, action had been taken. So I waited..

And waited, and waited. Another month went by I telephone the physiotherapy department. "Sorry, nothing in your name." I turned to my husband and got straight on the telephone to find out where this letter had gone to. The Neurology Department was very helpful on this occasion. I actually got the person who said she got the consultant to sign the letter. Leave it with me, I will get the physiotherapy department to telephone you.

Yes, they did within half an hour a polite lady came to phone who I have since met. The earliest I can get you in for assessment is January. I explained how long I had been waiting, but there was nothing before. January soon came. I went along for the assessment and what I did not realise was how much sensitivity I had lost on my left side. The walking was still not good, the weight bearing was not good and the knee was not good. Oh, the arm I forget to say at this point, I could not raise it above my head or in front of me. So all in all not good; however, the next six months would see changes at last. I was determined to work hard and follow the exercises. I met a lovely team of Physiotherapist who were empathetic but determined to get better movement. They have really kept me sane for the past six months. So thank you all, you know who you are.

We worked hard between us, regular appointments, daily exercise; two weeks lifting leg and getting much more movement with my arm. 1-1 sessions meant that my needs could be tweaked accordingly. I even went onto Virtual Rehab which is an amazing set of exercises/games made just for physiotherapy patients; there are not many hospitals with this. This can be adjusted according to the patients needs; I hope it is ok by the makers to mention this name, and to say this is great!

I was kept working with this and at the end of May 2016 it was decided that I should have a six weeks group session in the gymnasium. No, I was not swinging on bars; but learning how to balance, walk and increase muscle strength. The team won't mind me saying they were task masters. But with perseverance I got to a year after my stroke.

The head pain is more controlled the strength in my leg and arm is much better. I still get tired and have to rest, but all in all I am feeling good about myself. I am now going on with Physiotherapy another six weeks of Virtual Rehab and then Hydrotherapy. (You may ask 'have I tried swimming recently?' Yes, it is a little hard getting in but once in I can swim, only for about 20 minutes with stops because I get so tied. So 20 minutes swimming and an hour lay down, but at least I can.

So I am pleased to say feeling more positive. As long as I keep taking pills and exercise, I do believe this has helped immensely. One year on, not 100% but at least sixty-five, which is such an improvement believe you me. My advice is however you are feeling keep trying and believe that there is light at the end of a long tunnel.

NOTES

Chris Bennett

Chris Bennett

_____

_____

_____

_____

_____

_____

_____

_____

_____

_____

Teaching 2013

Mick and I in Majorca April, 2015 (before Stroke)

Malta 2015

With Seth May 2015 - before Stroke

With Seth June 2015 before my Stroke

Mick and I Malta August, 2015

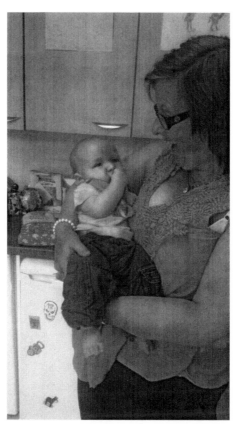

Me and Seth August 2015 (before flare)

With Clare December 31st 2015

With Henry January, 2016

Stroke Walk May 2016_ Image 1

June 2016, Ladies Day Ascot at club

Clare and I July 2016

Clare and Colin's Wedding reception hogroast

Gemma and I (Gemma's sunburnt)

Malta in pool before flair

Mick who has always been there for me.

Mick with Martyn and Tracey.

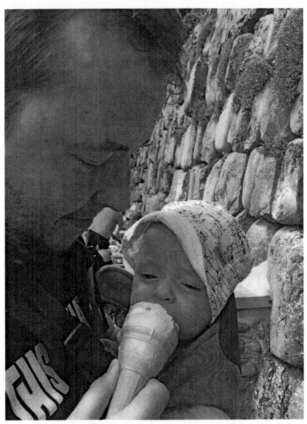

Mike (Dad) with Henry

My only sibling Lesley

Peter and Lesley

CHAPTER 5
THE JOURNEY

To get to this point a year on, I need to say that changes become slower, things are more noticeable. For instance touch me down my spine I will jump a mile. I could not believe this sensitivity. I had never had any back problems before. So why now? A question for my Neurologist when I see him.

There are three places on my back which are considerably tender (my husband can press and identify all three. But I can walk further, with a stick, because my left knee tends to give away but my balance is so much better. Ask the Physiotherapists. I am just so grateful for their support. Do I still need them oh yes! I even got their Virtual program working on the computer the other week. I am sorry to say three men could not even get this to work. The young student came in and pushed the lead and said 'it flickered'. Any Technicians at the hospital, I asked, but I just pulled the scart lead and pushed it back in and there it all started working. I will say no more.

By the way I can still drive better than I can walk, but I have a disabled badge which has helped me immensely. I can park nearer to entrances. I still get tired, but find I can pull over and grab a drink and carry on.

Still after about two hours that is enough. Once I asked a fellow stroke victim; "how is it I get so tired when I drive, but my concentration means I can blot out pain, numbness, pins and needles etc."

His reply was because we are concentrating on one thing and all our energy goes into one thing, that's why we get so tired. This seems a reasonable answer.

The days pass, some days I need more rest than others. I always have a low period within the day around 2pm. My face will look drawn I can feel my whole side pulling, my foot dragging and my eyes closing. I know I cannot drive when I am like this.

When I awake in the morning it still takes me about an hour to become fully alert. I often sit with a cup of tea and watch the news events before breakfast. This gets my body/brain alert and I can then get about 4 hours before I feel really tied again. Although, as any stroke victim will tell you, if it's not your lip not working right, it's your arm or other limbs feeling heavy and dragging in the morning.

After afternoon sleep I can then carry on another 4 hours, as long as I don't exert myself too much. After sessions of physiotherapy, always around lunchtime/ afternoon I am shattered! I need to rest.

This is noticeably longer than usual. This clearly takes it out of me but has been proving to improve muscle weakness. Yes, I do exercise every day but this clearly does make me tied.

The legs coming up higher, the arm is being lifted, I have more movement. If anyone says to me again it is still early days I will scream!

I keep being asked to compare how I was six months again, a month ago but I still have this wood pecker in my head that continues to tap constantly. Emotionally I would hope to say I am more in control, albeit the tablets. I am still anxious about having another but set myself a task, goal, challenge. The task could be simply vacuum cleaning (a lot slower than it was before the stroke). A goal, walk around a shop holding onto a trolley. A challenge, looking forward towards the future, telling others; through this book, talks, stroke group and public meetings. I am determined to share my story and help others along the way. We will see dear reader.

The journey continues, not as a marathon but a slow progression; movements, confidence and building self-esteem. Believe that things will get better and explain to others so they know how you are feeling post stoke. I know I probably upset family along the way; firstly not knowing what was happening to me, the realisation of the Stoke and coming to terms with the condition; which does not just affect you, but everyone around you. Their support means my journey can continue. Thank you; it has been a hell of a journey so far.

NOTES

Chris Bennett

_____

_____

_____

_____

_____

_____

_____

_____

_____

_____

_____

Chris Bennett

CHAPTER 6
EMOTIONS

The tears flood, the hankies are wet and putting on that brave face. Getting angry and frustrated when you can't do the simplest of jobs, like doing up a pair of shoes. How did you ever put up with me Mick? (and he still says he loves me). The stroke group helped him immensely. Talking to other halves to see how they are coping. I still wake him up in the night when I turn over. We take each day and when I get low he still does the Monty Python song. Thanks for being with me Mick. (I love you).

We just celebrated our thirty fifth wedding anniversary (Coral), we went away and we were waited on and sat in the warm evenings with a glass of wine. If you are wondering dear readers I would marry him again tomorrow. I am so sorry for what I put him through with my stroke.

Emotions run high all round my dearest Sister, Lesley does not know if she is coming or going, they have been so worried about me. My message to her is 'I am not quite back to normal whatever normal is, but I am getting there.' Thank you for being a caring big sister! To Peter her other half enabling me and supporting me to reach my goals! Thank you.

Do I say the right thing? Some days I will say something and say I did not mean that. But it is nothing nasty I hope. My Grandchildren are pleased to be getting their Nanny back. The oldest one Ben said 'Nanny I do understand, I knew what happened to you, but I will help'. Isabelle was just so pleased that I could do this dance on her dance machine with her. The younger two Seth and Henry, they have a Nanny who they both call and recognise. They are all lovely and keep me motivated. As do all of our children. Michelle, Clare, Gemma and Mike and of course there other halves who we will always have a laugh and joke with. I am just so grateful for all of their support. I know it has been an emotional journey for all of them.

To our dear friends whom emotions always run high with: Martyn and Tracey. We laugh, dance and drink a little and cry. Tracey is just so pleased to witness how well I am getting on and help me along the way. We are both grateful to you both.

I have spoken to my friends at the Stroke club who all get emotional about talking about their stroke, day-to-day living and feeling angry and frustrated. We all support one another, which is so nice. Knowing they understand and telling you, your looking good is an enormous ego boaster. My thanks and now my support goes to them. I cherish each day and want you all to know; I now want to help others with their emotional journey.

CHAPTER 7
WHAT'S NEXT

- *continue recovery*

- *support others*

- *except who I am*

- *build self-esteem*

Anyone who has faced death and continued to develop with life expectancy would probably say each day at a time. That is what I intend for the future. Enjoy the moments, treasure memories and build on recovery.

Recovery is not going to happen overnight. Acceptance is beginning to happen. This happened to me; the how I have shared the why still not sure. The acceptance of day-to-day and place realistic goals. Sometimes our children say things do you remember, they have a vivid recollection and it is not everything I forget, but it does annoy me when I clearly have no recollection. I am sorry but I remember the important things and treasure these memories.

I am beginning to take a more supportive role at our Stroke Club by becoming an adult workforce stroke group volunteer. Which is a pleasure, to befriend others and talk about their stroke and share/support their emotions. I have a friend from the stroke group, who I am supporting with her writing and getting her to hold the pen and form letters. She was unable to manipulate her hand effectively to hold the pen and share my Teaching/ career with others. Small achievements but I feel I can help others.

I hope this supportive role will help me look at who I am and except that I am getting better but slowly. This should support self-esteem and allow me to become less reliant on anti-depressants and believe in myself, once again.

NOTES

_____

_____

_____

_____

_____

_____

_____

_____

_____

_____

_____

_____

_____

_____

_____

_____

_____

_____

_____

_____

_____

_____

CHAPTER 8
I AM LUCKY!

How are you? The immortal words or "you are looking well." Do you know if anyone says the later I just want to scream! You might think I look well but my head is banging, I have pains up and down my leg and arm, my face is dragging and I feel like shit! Pardon the phrase. "Well," I say (with a deep breath, pause), "I am getting there," comes the reply with a smile. When really I just want to blurt out the way I am feeling. I know people are being polite and they are generally concerned. As my husband keeps singing, the notorious 'Monty Python' tribute; "always look on the bright side of life," I know he is trying to get me to smile, and he has at times got me to sing with tears running down my face! He is trying to help bless him and as I mentioned before he has been a great carer, comforter, dresser, great at cooking etc... along with our family and friends, who have always been there for support. So who I am and where I am is down to them. Some days my husband cannot stop me talking and another he is trying to make me laugh what a roller coaster!

It really hit home again two months ago when I was sent to see a different Neurologist. You have had a brain injury as I heard those words the tears ran down my face. The block was released but some damage would have been done. I explained how I was feeling. He said I was suffering from 'Post-Traumatic Stress Syndrome.' I had gone through a life changing experience, I explained about my fear of having another. He said you will feel like this for a while but there are tablets that can calm the anxiety.

I have never liked taking anti-depressants, but they have been the best thing ever. When I know I am ready I will talk with the Doctor about decreasing my dose. Until then I seem to have more control, make decisions etc.

Post stoke I have noticed my literacy, word skills still appear to be good. However, I have noticed my maths skills are poor; considering I used to teach top maths set in Primary, hay-ho! Adding up double figures in my head is really hard, I find I have to write numbers down in a sum and add up that way, taking away is just as hard and multiplication is not as quick. By the way I am trying to retrain my brain. I play Scrabble with my husband. They always say 'never play with a Teacher!' The difference is I know the words but I have forgotten the meaning. I am sure in time the pathways in my brain will sort themselves out. In the meantime, I will play word games, do the scoring to improve maths, read and write and absorb as much knowledge as possible.

This Stroke has enabled me to meet so many people, both professional and make new friends. I am so grateful to them all 'Thank you!' for listening to me and keeping me sane! Well, I try. Next for me, who knows what opportunities I will succumb, but all as I know, is that 'I am Lucky!'

Lucky to be alive!

Lucky to have such caring people around me!

And Lucky that I can tell my story!

THANK YOU TO YOU ALL!

NOTES

Chris Bennett

_____

_____

_____

_____

_____

_____

_____

_____

_____

_____

_____

Chris Bennett

_____

_____

_____

_____

_____

_____

_____

_____

_____

_____

Lightning Source UK Ltd.
Milton Keynes UK
UKOW02f1404251016
286091UK00002B/427/P